How to Grow Orchids

Phalaenopsis amabilis

How to Grow Orchids

A Beginner's Guide to Growing Orchids

by
Fran Barnwell

Published by: Rowan House Publishing

First Printing: 2012

4

Contents

List of Illustrations

Introduction: What's so Special About Orchids?

Figure 1 *Laelia jongheana*

Orchids have long held a fascination for me, with their exotic appearance and their fabulous colours. But I was also well aware of their reputation for being difficult to grow at home. Eventually, however, I could no longer resist, and once I started to understand the basics of orchid care, I was hooked.

Without a doubt, there are some plants in the orchid family that are extremely difficult to care for, but there are many, many others whose needs are easily met by the home grower.

And this is what this book is about, to help you and me, people who are fascinated by orchids, but perhaps, because we don't quite understand their needs, are wary of buying orchids for the home.

Some notes about orchids

Next to the rose, orchids are the most in-demand flowers, both for individuals as house plants and within the commercial marketplace for cut flowers, in particular as wedding flowers. In addition, no plant family has as many different flowers as the orchid family. And given that orchids are known to grow in most parts of the world, with the exception of Antarctica, you begin to realise that we are talking about a truly exceptional plant.

Their variety is quite staggering: some orchids grow only one flower on each stem, while others can have more than a hundred blooms on a single spike with amazing variations in colours: from white, yellow through to pink and purple and multi-coloured.

There is one orchid genus, however, that is also commercially important, other than for the value of its flowers, and that is the Vanilla orchid, which is used as a flavouring, and indeed is the source of vanilla. And, of course, the scent of orchids is frequently used by perfumers.

The earliest written evidence of orchids is in the form of Chinese and Japanese drawing and literature as long ago as circa 700 BC. In the past, the orchid was believed to have healing powers and, in many cultures, was used as a herbal or natural remedy.

Orchids are also one of the most adaptable plant groups on earth, and mainly fall into two types: the terrestrial orchid, which grows on the ground, though some terrestrial species also have aerial roots as well as underground roots, and the epiphytes orchid, which grows in trees, or on rocks, in their natural habitat.

Both tropical and sub-tropical orchids are available at nurseries and through orchid clubs throughout the world, and are even now readily available in some supermarkets. There are also quite a few orchids that grow in colder climates, although these may be more difficult to find.

One of the best places to see the wide range of orchids is at The National Orchid Garden in Singapore, now considered by some to have the finest collections of orchids in cultivation that is open to the public.

Orchids have become a major market throughout the world. Buyers bid hundreds of dollars on new or improved hybrids and, as mentioned earlier, they are now one of the most popular cut flowers on the market. Although orchid hybridisation has been taking place for many years, it is only recently that new technology has turned this business into the success it is today.

Growing orchids can be a wonderfully rewarding activity, but for many years it was thought that orchids were far too difficult for amateur growers to grow indoors. However, if you can provide the living conditions they need, it is perfectly possible to have a stunning orchid flower display in your home.

The three main requirements for the orchid to bloom are the right amounts of water, light, and heat. The plant receives moisture through its roots, as with all other plants, and thrives in bright, indirect sunlight. In addition, the plants need to be provided with enough humidity and air flow.

It is important, therefore, that you decide where you will place your new orchid before you actually buy one, as they are not keen on being moved around too much.

Orchids can provide enormous pleasure to those who grow them, and once you have tried growing this wonderful plant, I am sure you will also become hooked!

In this book, I am going to focus on growing those orchids that are the easiest to obtain and to look after, but will also be providing information on the less common orchids, so that you can understand more about these plants and, hopefully, this will encourage you to expand your collection.

Overview of the book

In the next chapter, I will be looking at a few of the many species of orchids that are among the most popular and explain a little about where they come from and their care. I have also included a few of the not-so-common orchids and their characteristics.

In the following two chapters, I will go into more details about orchid care. I will explain about an orchid's needs for light, heat and humidity, as well as what they require in the form of watering, fertiliser and the importance of rest.

Next, I will look at another important aspect of caring for orchids and that is how to re-pot your orchid and the potting materials to use. I follow this with a chapter on the propagation of orchids, in other words, how to increase your stock of orchids, which I am sure every orchid lover would love to be able to do. Lastly, I will look at the pests and diseases that can affect orchids grown indoors and how best to deal with them.

Throughout the book are photographs and plates that will give you an idea of just how varied the appearance of some orchid flowers can be.

If you are really keen to get going with your orchid growing, I provide a summary of the most popular orchids and their basic needs in a Quick Reference Guide at the back of the book. But if you do go straight to this section, please go back and read the whole book when you have more time!

I have also provided a Glossary of a some of the more common terms used, as well as an Acknowledgements section, which provides information on the origins of the illustrations.

In the book, I have occasionally referred to aspects of growing orchids that may seem quite technical, or terminology that is hard to understand. Where this happens, I have done my best to explain it in layman's terms.

Enjoy your orchids, they are a spectacular family of flowers!

Figure 2 *Epidendrum pallidiflorum*

Where to Start: Discover the Orchid Family

Figure 3 *Phalaenopsis, or 'moth' orchid*

In this chapter, I am going to give you an outline of the different types of orchid and, in particular, my aim is to help you decide which ones you would like to grow. And without a doubt, there are some that are easier than others. But this will give you a broad and general view of the subject in the hope that you will be encouraged to investigate further, although it is not intended to be a complete list nor provide a scientific description.

As mentioned in the Introduction, there are many, many different species and hybrids of orchids, but first, we are going to look at the main types of orchids.

Terrestrial, semi-terrestrial, epiphytic

The terrestrial orchids, as the word implies, are species that grow on the ground and are found in the temperate zones of both hemispheres. They are among some of the most popular orchids and although terrestrial orchids have roots that grow beneath the surface of the soil just as with most other kinds of plants, some terrestrial orchids are also semi-terrestrial: they have both underground and aerial roots.

Cymbidium orchids are a terrestrial orchid that has 40 species and thousands of hybrids and they were among one of the first species of orchids to be cultivated. They are a great example of terrestrials that not only grow on the ground but can also grow on trees and rocky ground and can be found from South-east Asia to Japan and also in

Australia. Cymbidium orchids are so popular because they are easy to grow and are therefore a perfect choice for beginners, plus, with the proper care, they will provide beautiful flowers every year.

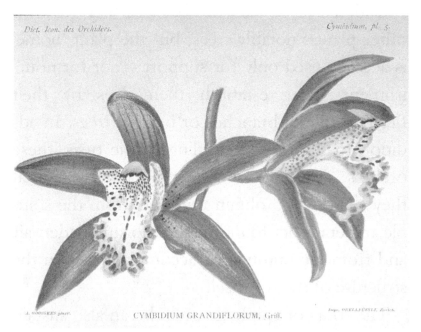

Figure 4 *Cymbidium grandiflorum*

By far the largest and most varied of the orchid family are included in the semi-terrestrial and epiphytic groups. These are tropical or subtropical plants, living on trees in the rain-swept coastal jungles or on bare rocks in the hot sun. Their elevation ranges from sea level to two thousand feet above sea level, and they grow well throughout parts of Asia, the islands of the South Pacific, Australia, New Zealand, Africa, and South and Central America.

The epiphytic orchids are widely, yet wrongly, considered to be parasites because they grow on other plants, notably trees, but the plant 'home' is actually used only for support – not for nourishment. They establish themselves by their fleshy roots on branches or bark of trees. In addition to the roots that cling to the trees, these orchids also have aerial (epiphytic) roots that they send out to obtain nutrients from the soluble mineral salts found in the moisture-laden air and from the humus that accumulates within the structure of the tree itself.

The roots of epiphytic orchids can also sustain the plant through both wet and dry periods as the tough, stringy core of the root is surrounded by a spongy off-white covering that can absorb water easily. When it rains, this cover soaks up water, turning pale green when it is completely saturated. The orchid's roots retain this moisture and will release it gradually to the plant tissues.

There are also some species of epiphytic orchids that can be found clinging to rocks. As they are suspended from trees or rocks, the epiphytes thrive in filtered light and always in open situations with plenty of air flow – a point to note when caring for your own orchids.

Figure 5 *Epiphytic orchids in the wild*

Dendrobiums are the best known epiphytes orchid. Although they are easy to grow, they require slightly more care than Cymbidiums and do not flower as easily on a regular basis. There are over 1,000 species of Dendrobiums and are found in the natural tropical conditions of Northern India, South-east Asia, Australia and

Polynesia. They therefore thrive in warm, humid growing conditions and should be kept moist.

Another popular epiphyte type of orchid is the Phalaenopsis, which is easy to grow and has long-lasting flowers. These orchids are often used for wedding decorations, for example, in corsages, and have a wide range of colours including pinks, yellows, and even stripes.

There is a further classification of orchids that I want to cover, which refers to their growth habit, and that is...

Monopodial and sympodial groups

The monopodial, of which Vanda is an example, grows continuously from a central crown, which eventually appears above a long stem that has frequently lost its lower leaves. Phalaenopsis, although monopodial, is stemless but, each year, grows a pair of leaves from the distinctive crown.

The leaves of monopodial orchids are heavy, leathery, fleshy, and capable of storing some quantity of moisture, but the plants must never be allowed to dry out completely.

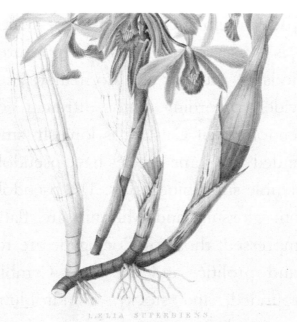

Figure 6 *Laelia, showing sympodial growth*

The sympodial group, of which Cattleya, Laelia and Coelogyne are notable examples, has a creeping rootstock, with each new growth springing from the base and alongside the last year's growth (see Figure 6).

The new growth appears as a swelling or 'dormant' eye that, at the proper time, will 'break' or begin to grow. In some genera, such as Coelogyne, the growths will break in several directions, but in Cattleya usually in only one.

The pseudobulb, a characteristic of sympodial orchids, is a reservoir for food and moisture during periods of drought and dormancy, and can differ widely according to the different genera. The pseudobulb of Cattleya is longish, smooth, and rounded and some species have pseudobulbs that resemble small pineapples. The pseudobulbs of Odontoglossum and Miltonia are flattened and compressed; those of Coelogyne are round, short, and prolific; and those of Cymbidium large, rounded, and stocky. Dendrobium, in many species, lacks pseudobulbs, but even the long cane-like flower stems, along which the leaves grow in pairs, are capable of storing food and moisture.

Different orchid species

Now, let's look at the different species of orchids in more detail. I'll start with the better known and more popular orchids.

The **Cattleya** (KAT-lee-a), much loved by the florist and valuable for breeding large and showy hybrids, is one of the top favourites amongst orchid growers.

There are over 40 species of Cattleya and, in the wild, these plants grow in thick clusters on trees.

Figure 7 *Cattleya intermedia*

The Cattleya is composed of longish, rounded pseudobulbs, which advance, rhizome-fashion, along the surface of the potting mixture, and are topped by one, two, or three long green leaves, which are firm and leathery in texture. The average Cattleya grows one new pseudobulb a year. After several new bulbs have been formed, the old ones tend to lose their leaves and roots, becoming back-bulbs.

These back-bulbs are frequently referred to as 'poor relations', owing to their habit of sapping the energy from the plant. However, if they are removed and placed in a warm, moist spot they will often respond by putting on new growth and roots to start a new plant!

A tiny swelling or dormant eye can be found at the base of each pseudobulb in a Cattleya plant. The eye of the youngest bulb will begin to swell and break into growth, acquiring new leaves and sending out new roots. A new pseudobulb is formed and, in a healthy, well-cared-for plant, each will be finer and larger than the last.

From among the leaves at the top of the new growth, the flower sheath will form. Species differ in the length of time required for maturing or flowering.

The Cattleya is among the larger of the species orchids – species meaning 'natural' as opposed to 'hybrid', and often crossed with Laelia, a very similar plant in look and habit, to produce Laelio-cattleya hybrids. The colours of these orchids ranges through all shades and tints of purple, from amethyst and violet to magenta and deep red. Brown, yellow, and green species are also found. Many of the species have 'alba' varieties, whose flowers are pure white with a touch of green or yellow at the throat.

The genus **Phalaenopsis** (fal-en-OP-sis) – more commonly known as 'moth orchid' and sometimes 'butterfly orchid' – not only has beautiful flowers but also smooth, shiny, large leaves, coming from the central crown. In recent years they have often replaced lily-of-the-valley for bridal bouquets because of the purity of their white spray-like flowers (see Figure 3 above). Heavy strap-like roots spread out to search for moisture and, owing to their habit of roving and clinging to foreign objects, can often cause a problem when re-potting (more on this later). Erect woody stems bear prolific flowers until the weight causes them to curve gracefully.

The structure of the flowers is quite beautiful, the top sepal rounded, shaping to a point at the top; the side petals broad and sweeping; the two lower sepals, narrower and sometimes overlapping, form a background for the remarkable lip. Red lines in the throat seem to signal the way for pollinating insects, and the front lobes of the lip are frequently elongated into curling tendrils.

The genus **Dendrobium** (den-DROH-bee-um) is prolific and diverse, comprising some 100 species, with a wide variety of size and shape. It can be found from southern Asia, through Ceylon, Malaya, Siam, China, Japan, throughout the Philippines, Java, Sumatra, Borneo, to Australia and New Zealand. They can grow on trees, in the ground, and on bare rocks, as well as through extremes of temperature and altitude.

The Dendrobium plant has an unusual appearance: it is sympodial, epiphytic, and bulbless, and has heavy cane-like stems, which also produce the papery green leaves. These canes store sufficient moisture and food to keep the plant alive through periods of extreme drought.

The genus is divided into deciduous and evergreen, which again divides into warm- and cool-growing plants. All evergreen Dendrobiums are attractive plants with graceful, leafy foliage. They have cane-like stems, taking the place of pseudobulbs, and bear the flowers in erect panicles (clusters), singly at the nodes, or in drooping racemes (stems with flowers attached at intervals).

Figure 8 *Dendrobium devonianum*

Deciduous Dendrobiums, once the leaves have dropped off each year, are peculiar-looking plants, with dry and shrivelled bamboo-like canes. It is always a surprise, and more lovely by contrast, when the flowers bud and bloom from the joints, or nodes, of these dry canes. Deciduous Dendrobiums bloom on the old wood, and evergreen Dendrobiums on the new growth.

The genus **Oncidium** (on-SID-ee-um) is a very old one, as well being one of the most diverse, and come in more than 1,000 variations of shape, size and colour. It ranges from hot coastal regions to the cold of altitudes up to 12,000 feet and is native to Mexico, Central and tropical South America, and the West Indies. It has short, thick pseudobulbs and slender, graceful leaves. Though the flowers are genrally small compared to, for example, the Cattleya, they are a spray-type of considerable grace and charm. The blooms are flat, of silky texture, and often referred to as 'dancing ladies'. The clear bright yellow flowers are outstanding.

Figure 9 *Oncidium or 'dancing ladies'*

Paphiopedilums (paff-ee-oh-PED-ih-lum) are both evergreen and deciduous. The deciduous groups are from South America and are chiefly of specialised botanical interest. All of North America boasts Paphiopedilums, but not many people are aware that the modest 'lady's slipper' and 'moccasin flower' are orchids, and unassuming relatives of the magnificent Cattleya. Paphiopedilums are to be found in some form practically all over the world.

More showy, and adaptable to greenhouse culture, the tropical Paphiopedilum, natives of the Far East, are handsome plants with shiny dark green foliage. These warmer-growing types have attractively mottled leaves and they are the parents of the rounded-petal hybrids so prized by florists.

Figure 10 *Paphiopedilum or 'slipper' orchid*

Paphiopedilum in its tropical forms is a genus highly recommended for new orchid growers as it is adaptable and easy to grow indoors.

The genus **Cymbidium** (sim-Bid-ee-em) is a hardy one, achieving well-deserved popularity. These plants are sympodial, terrestrial, semi-terrestrial, and epiphytic. They are grown outdoors in the tropics and thrive particularly on the west coast of the USA, where southern California hopes to become the Cymbidium centre of the world!

The plants have great solid pseudobulbs and very long grass-like leaves. From the depths of this graceful foliage (waist high), the flowers climb along tall, sturdy stems, usually erect, but drooping in some species. This handsome spray orchid has lent itself so well to hybridising that it can rival, in size and shape, that of the Cattleya, with an amazing range of colour.

Species of Cymbidium have proved rather difficult to grow under artificial conditions, probably owing to the difficulty of giving them proper ventilation. For that reason, as well as for their superior beauty and size, the hybrids are far better known than the species. They must be grown in a cool house or outdoors. Although there are 60 known species, only about 10 of them have been used to any extent in making the many lovely hybrids.

The genus **Vanda** contains many species, represented by large handsome plants and a wide range of beautiful flowers. Some growers consider these plants difficult to cultivate, but their charm is well worth the effort of providing their particular needs. The plants are pseudobulb-less, the leaves distichous (dis-tik-ous), or disposed in two parallel lines along the heavy, erect stem.

Figure 11 *Vanda, showing monopodial growth*

The tendency of the stem is to grow up toward the sun, and can surprise new orchid growers when they find the plant reaching the roof, with no more room to grow. The lower leaves frequently drop off. Thick aerial roots form along the stem and, when smooth, green-tipped, and fat, are an indication that the plant is healthy. When they become shrivelled and ringed, something has gone very wrong with their care.

34

In the showier species, the flowers are borne in loose racemes and have spreading sepals and petals; in others the petals are spread and tend to roll under. In the former type, the texture of the flowers is papery. In the latter the texture is leathery or waxy and very heavy. The lip is often very inconspicuous.

Epidendrum (ep-i-DEN-drum) is a hardy genus to which belong a great number of so-called 'botanicals' that, because their flowers are small and of no commercial value, are of interest only to botanists. The plant is vine-like in some species, but has definite pseudobulbs in others; it is epiphytic and sympodial.

The small flowers are very abundant, usually starry – slender sepals and petals as contrasted with the broad petals and sepals of, for example, Phalaenopsis – and frequently of brilliant colouring, including all shades of red from orange to maroon. It grows like a weed in Mexico and often as hedging. Plants have pseudobulbs of many and varied shapes.

And here are a few more of the lesser-known orchids…

Sophronitis (sof-row-NYE-tis) is a genus of epiphytic, dwarf, evergreen plants similar in appearance and habit to Cattleya but requiring cooler conditions and more light. The colouring of the flowers is brilliant.

Members of the genus **Odontoglossum** (oh-dont-oh-GLOS-um) can be difficult to grow under artificial cultivation, as they require conditions entirely different from those of most greenhouse orchids. Seldom found at an elevation of less than 5,000 feet, they need shade, air, and moisture without being chilled. They are so eye-catching and lovely, however, that it can be well worth the effort to study their native environment and supply conditions to make them happy.

The plants are small, compact, evergreen, sympodial, and epiphytic, and the flowers are borne along tall, curving spikes. The species are many and varied, all beautiful.

Stanhopea (stan-HOPE-ee-ah) is an interesting genus. It is epiphytic and sympodial, with large, dramatic, fragrant flowers, and has the habit of throwing the flower spike from the bottom of the plant, so that it requires potting in a basket.

The flowers are not prolific; they do have a peculiar waxy texture but are disappointingly short-lived, but if they are cut immediately and placed in water they can last a little longer. The fleshy prominent lip and organs for reproduction display many surprising shapes in the different species. The plants are pseudobulbous and have dark green leaves.

The genus **Miltonia** has very fragile-looking plants and the pseudobulbs are such a pale green that they appear transparent. The delicate foliage closely clings to the pseudobulbs at the base and feathering out at the top. The plants are difficult to maintain without yellowing or spotting, and are very susceptible to red spider-mites, whose inroads still further disfigure their appearance. They are epiphytic and sympodial.

The flowers are large for the size of the bulb and are borne in large numbers on a slender, erect stem. Because of its beauty and variety, it can be a desirable plant for an amateur collection. The flowers do not last well when cut, but if left on the plant are long-lived. If well-tended, the whole plant makes a graceful and attractive decoration or centrepiece.

The genus **Phaius** (FAY-us), although not one of the treasured 'commercials', is satisfactory and easy to grow. The plant is terrestrial and epiphytic, handsomely ornamental, and usually pseudobulbous. It has large fine leaves from the middle of which rise tall, erect stems bearing large, showy flowers.

The colouring can be unusual with the frequent combination of white and yellow, while the outside of the petals, sepals, and lip is white.

The genus **Calanthe** (ca-LAN-thee) is terrestrial, infrequently epiphytic, sympodial, evergreen, and sometimes deciduous. Having large, wide, gracefully drooping leaves of shimmering texture, it has often, in the past, been used for table decoration.

The pseudobulbs are large, heavy, and of light olive-green, and the flowers grow in sprays and are delicately coloured, though coarser in texture than most orchids.

Coelogyne (see-LOJ-in-ee) is a pseudobulbous, evergreen, sympodial epiphyte. It varies considerably with the species, the bulbs of C. *cristate* being short, plump, and well-rounded, while those of C. *pan-durata* are flattened, compressed, and distichous.

The flowers are oddly attractive and of crisp texture, growing freely on racemes coming from the centre of the new growths, and usually having sepals broader than the smaller petals.

The genus **Lycaste** (lye-KASS-tee) is a sympodial epiphyte, attractive and easy to grow. It has thick pseudobulbs and short, ribbed leaves, and in some species the flowers are extremely large for the size of the plant.

There is a wide colour range, from deep pink to greenish-brown; the texture is exquisite; and the shape is rather like a half-open rosebud. It is strictly a native of the tropical western hemisphere.

Cycnoches (SIK-no-keez) is a lovely genus that has been neglected by many growers. The plants have heavy, woody pseudobulbs. The graceful foliage is frequently shed in the winter and the plant produces large, handsome flowers whose shape has earned it the beautiful name of 'swan's neck orchid'.

The flowers are so unusual and lovely that they are worth any amount of labour involved in encouraging them to bloom. However, a big disadvantage is that flowering is such a strain on the plant that the old bulb often gives all its strength to the new growth, and then shrivels and dies.

Catasetum (kat-a-SEE-tum) is a genus that is of special interest not because of its beauty, but because of the weird shape of its flowers and the amazing contrivances used in pollination. It is seldom seen in collections. It is definitely epiphytic, producing aerial roots in profusion; it is sympodial and native to Central America.

When the plant was originally found, it was thought that the male flower-producing plant and the female were two separate species. Green, yellow, and brown predominate in the colour scheme of these flowers.

Figure 12 *Catasetum macrocarpum*

Masdevallia (mas-de-VAL-lee-a) is a large genus, which is remarkable principally for the weird and fantastic shape taken by its flowers. It is native to tropical America. It is sympodial and both terrestrial and epiphytic. Its creeping rhizome and shiny leaves take the place of pseudobulbs. The flowers resemble unearthly insects, with long, tapering, curled sepals and a tubular or contorted lip, which is most frequently white.

And finally…

Vanilla: it may surprise and interest newcomers to orchids that Vanilla is a genus of the orchid family. It is exceedingly difficult to grow, however, owing to its wandering, vine-like habit of growth, and it flowers infrequently in the temperate zone. It is monopodial, epiphytic, and evergreen. It lacks pseudobulbs, but has heavy, fleshy leaves. The flowers are fairly large, but the plant must assume considerable size before it will flower. The seed pods are, of course, the source of vanilla extract flavouring.

Let's summarise

As you can see from the above, there are many wonderful plants to choose from, with many varied flower shapes, and that is only the tip of the orchid iceberg! But I have purposely kept my list to those orchids that are generally considered to be the most suitable for a beginner to grow, as well as those that are readily available from orchid nurseries.

And I would highly recommend that you make your first choice from those listed above, after all, once you have success with one plant, you are more likely to move on to attempt to grow more challenging plants. But if your first efforts fail, then sadly, it would be all too easy to give up.

But in addition, which orchids you grow very much depends on the growing conditions you can provide for the plant, as their needs can differ widely. And in the next chapter, I will be covering the various conditions under which orchids thrive.

Figure 13 *Masdevallia schroderiana*

What an Orchid Needs

Figure 14 *Sophronitis coccinea*

The growth and development of an orchid can be quite complicated and can vary from species to species but, for the new grower, a basic grasp of the plant's requirements will be sufficient to maintain the health, growth and flowering of the plant. The rewards, of course, are spectacular.

Now for the technical bit: using the energy provided by light, the green leaf chlorophyll of the plant transforms the carbon dioxide from the air, as well as the mineral salts from moisture, into sugar and other carbohydrates. These energy carbohydrates are stored until needed, either for rebuilding plant tissue or for flowering. The pseudobulbs of some types, the large leathery leaves of others, and the slender grass-like leaves of orchids lacking pseudobulbs are used as storage reservoirs.

There are no hard and fast rules to follow, and the three elements of light, heat and humidity will vary dependent on the plant and the season. In many cases, knowing where the plants grow in their natural habitat can be helpful to understand their needs.

But there are some important points to note and we will start off by looking at the plants' light requirements.

Light

There are two methods of using light for orchids and this can be either 'soft' or 'hard'. The term 'soft' means that the plant is shaded from the sun so that the leaves produced are a beautiful dark green. The down side of this is that it can have an adverse effect on the quality of the flowers. And care must be taken not to provide so much shade that you slow down the actual growth of the plant.

To grow 'hard' means to allow as much light as possible, but in this case the leaves will look decidedly yellow. This method, while affecting the appearance of the plant, can however give increased blooms.

The claim that the 'hard' method of growing orchids increases flower growth would seem to make sense if we look at the conditions under which orchids grow in their natural state: the natural environment is one of bright light. But remember that, even for those varieties of orchid that grow in full sun, there is usually some cloud cover in their natural habitat, so too much direct sunlight must be avoided, since this will burn the plant and growth will be interrupted.

Whatever decision you make, one thing is important and that is you must be consistent in your treatment of your plant. Orchids are very susceptible to shock of any kind, such as, sudden changes in temperature or light levels, and they take considerable time to recover – if they ever do.

It is important to note that if more sun is provided, then more moisture and air will be required. If the plants are grown with minimum sun they will require less moisture, but always ensure a good flow of air.

A common mistake for anyone new to growing orchids is to increase the heat supplied to the plant during the winter. As the plant stores energy during daylight hours, and gives off energy at night, an increase in temperature will increase this release of energy.

During winter, of course, daylight hours are shorter which leaves the plant with less energy stored for growth, and losing more energy at night than can be stored during the day, can lead to a reduction in the health of the plant.

There is a further complication in that each species has its own light requirements, so we will now take a look at some of the most popular plants and see what they need in terms of light.

Cattleyas, native to Central and South America, are found hanging on trees in the tropical rain forests. The plants are protected from the burning midday sun by foliage directly overhead. This means that we can expose the Cattleya to the sun, but provide shade during the hotter parts of the day in summer. The increased exposure to sun needs a corresponding increase in humidity to prevent the pseudobulbs from shrivelling.

Also among the sun-worshipers are the Vandas, natives of India, the Philippines, and some Pacific islands. They will not thrive without adequate sun, and they must have corresponding amounts of heat and water. The evergreen Dendrobiums, native to the islands of South-east Asia, and Oncidiums, from Central and South America, are also sun-worshipers.

Phalaenopsis, the popular moth orchid, comes from the Philippines and the Eastern Archipelago. As they are shade plants, the moth orchids prefer dappled light (an east or west facing windowsill behind a net curtain is ideal). Too much bright light can burn the leaves and turn the plants yellowish while too little will result in plants with soft leaves that don't flower.

As a rule, orchids from mountainous regions or from the temperate zone need protection from direct sun. Cymbidiums, natives of the Himalayas, require controlled sun and cool conditions with abundant air. They enjoy the morning and afternoon sun most, but should be protected from the hot midday sun. A light green leaf with just a hint of yellow indicates the maximum amount of sun the plant can take, and a dark green leaf indicates not enough sun.

Odontoglossums, of South America, are normally found at heights of from 5,000 to 12,000 feet. They require cool, shaded conditions at all times and for this reason they are a little difficult to raise with other species.

Miltonias are found at heights up to 8,000 feet in Brazil, Costa Rica, and Colombia. They require shaded sunlight. Deciduous Dendrobiums, native to India and the Philippines, must be protected from the sun during the growing season.

Paphiopedilums, better known as 'lady's slipper' orchids, are found worldwide. They enjoy bright light but their leaves burn quickly with too much sun. Try protecting the plant from direct sunlight by positioning it behind another plant that needs the sun (Dendrobium, Cattleya or Oncidium). Sheer curtains will also take the edge off the hot sun, or place the plant in a north or east facing window. Generally the mottled-leaved types require more shade and more heat.

As a point of interest – and here are more technical bits – if you are looking for information about light requirements for your orchid, you may find that horticulturalists talk of lighting in terms of 'foot-candles', which is a measure of the intensity of light.

As an example, unobstructed full sunlight has a measurement of around 10,000 fc, whereas for an overcast day, it can reduce to around 1,000 fc. Light indoors coming through a window can range from as low as 100 fc up to 5,000 fc, depending on the direction the window faces, the weather outside, and how far or near the plant is to the window.

Heat

The amount of heat the plant requires is closely linked to the amount of light it receives. As in most native habitats, the temperature can be some degrees lower in winter than in summer.

To keep it simple, there are three temperature zones for orchids: warm, intermediate and cool:

Warm growers: prefer day-time temperatures around 70°–85°F (20°–30°C) but night-time temperature should not fall below around 65°F (18°C). Included in this group are Cattleyas, Dendrobiums, Phalaenopsis and Vandas.

Intermediate growers: these orchids, which include Oncidiums, Paphiopedilums and Epidendrums, need temperatures of between 60° and 75°F (15°–25°C) with a drop of around 10°F (5°C) at night.

Cool growers: this group includes Cymbidiums and Odontoglossums and they can take temperatures of 50°–70°F (10°–20°C) with a night-time temperature drop of around 15°F (8°C). Some, for example, Cymbidiums, can even tolerate temperatures as low as 40° (4°C).

All of these orchids, however, require the temperature drop at night indicated, which enables the plant's daily cycles of chemical changes to occur.

And in general, as you can see, the brighter the light requirement of the plant, the higher the temperature it needs.

Air flow and humidity

With regard to ventilation, we again find varying needs among orchids. The cooler-growing orchids require increased circulation and the warmer-growing orchids require less. A gentle circulation of air is ideal and strong draughts are to be avoided, particularly from open windows. More space around the plant will help air flow and it will quickly start to show signs of distress as a result of air that is too stagnant or dry.

And talking of dryness, during the winter, homes, especially those in cold climates with central heating systems, usually have a relative humidity of about 15 per cent. Because this is the average humidity found in most desert areas, you have to do something to raise the humidity to at least 50 per cent in order to keep orchids happy.

To increase the humidity level, it is a good idea to grow plants on top of a waterproof tray filled with pebbles. Add water to the tray so that the level is just below the surface of the pebbles, then put the plants on top of this bed of damp pebbles. Care is needed, however, to make sure that the pebbles are always kept clean to prevent an accumulation of pests or bacteria that might affect the plant. It is also important to make sure that the pot itself does not stand in the water, which would result in a waterlogged growing medium.

But light, heat and humidity are not the only conditions that the newbie orchid grower has to consider for their orchids. And in the next chapter we will be looking at other growing requirements.

More Orchid Needs

Figure 15 *Miltonia*

One of the major concerns of anyone new to orchid growing is the rather tricky question of how much do orchids need to be watered? As there appears to be some uncertainty and confusion on this matter, we are going to start off this second part of looking at orchid care with the subject of watering. In this chapter, I also want to look at the use of fertiliser for your orchids, which is

closely linked to watering, and then finally looking at the orchid's need for rest.

Water

As with other aspects of orchid care, there is a
wide variation in the watering needs of many
species. It is a common mistake to assume that
as many orchids are native to tropical rainforests,
they should be watered frequently. Unfortunate-
ly, over-watering kills the plants more often than
under-watering.

However, if you are in doubt as to how much
and how often to water, it is far better to give
less water than too much. Dryness will deter the
growth of the plant, but too much moisture will
kill it. If water remains in the pot and does not
dry out in a week or ten days, it is likely that the
roots will have rotted off. The pseudobulbs will
shrivel and the leaves droop.

It is easy to mistake this as an indication of
dryness, and treat the pot to another watering,
with the inevitable result of rotting the remaining
roots and probably killing the plant.

There is no one rule that works for orchids. Watering needs depend on the temperature, the humidity, and the type of potting medium. Therefore, plants needs to be checked for signs of dryness-like appearance; check the weight of the pot and, if needed, stick your finger into the medium! One way of making sure you have the watering balance right, is to check the roots of the plant: over-watered roots look brown and mushy; under-watered roots are a pale grey and dry looking. And the best advice is to check the condition of your plants as often as possible.

But there are a few general guidelines:

- And the first is no matter what kind of orchid you grow, it should never be allowed to sit in water.
- Always water in the morning: always. Night-time watering allows water to stagnate in the growing tips of Phalaenopsis or the flower sheaths of Cattleyas. This encourages bacterial and fungal diseases. Orchid plant leaves should be dry by nightfall.

- As a general rule, the higher the temperature, the more water the plant will need. But the higher the humidity, there is less need for water.

- And when you water, you can water thoroughly. Many home-growers sometimes submerge their plants, pots and all, into a bucket or sink of water for several minutes to make sure that the roots are completely saturated and rehydrated.

- The type of potting medium also affects how much water should be given, as the greater the water retention of the medium, the less often you will need to water.

How then do you treat the different types of orchid? If your orchid is a Cattleya, Oncidium or Dendrobium, it is a good idea to soak the pot thoroughly and then allow the potting material almost, but not completely, to dry out. The pots should not become completely dry since the bulbs may shrivel and plant growth would be arrested. When not in active growth, they require less water.

Vandas, since they are without pseudobulbs, must have water at all times, but their vigorous aerial roots will take care of some deficiency in watering by taking moisture from the air. Phalaenopsis, also pseudobulb-less, must not be allowed to dry out entirely. Watering of this species must be done with care to prevent water from remaining in the crowns, a condition that encourages the growth of fungus.

Cymbidiums should not be allowed to dry out. Standing pots on damp gravel on the floor seems to give them the warmth at the top and coolness at the base that they prefer. The potting mixture should be moist, well drained but not soggy. Paphiopedilum, Miltonia, and Odontoglossums also require moisture at their roots.

I also want to look at the importance of using an overhead spray. Orchids appreciate a fine spray as much as they do diffused light. A daily spray at the height of summer, or even two or more sprays a day will be gratefully received by your plant. But do ensure that you spray your plants early in the day to give the leaves a chance to dry before nightfall.

Finally, it is recommended that the plants have water with an acidity reading of approximately pH 4.5 to 5.

And in case you are interested, here are more technical bits: distilled water is neutral, being neither acid nor alkaline, and has been designated as pH 7 (pH – parts hydrogen), the number 7 representing this neutrality. Numbers above 7 denote increasing alkalinity; numbers below 7 increasing acidity. Water of 4.5 to 5 has sufficient acid content for orchids.

For a long time, serious growers insisted that orchids could only be watered with rain water. Nowadays, most people just use tap water, and this is fine. However, it could be that treated water may have higher salt content, and some water is high in calcium. Check to see if deposits form on your plants, and if so, then you may wish to look for a new water source.

If you are unsure about the alkalinity/acidity of your water supply, then I can recommend using rain water, as normal rain water has a pH somewhere between 4.3 and 5.6. Just make sure that any containers are clean and chemical free.

Fertilisers

Fertilising orchids, as with all plants, can help them grow and flower more, and is an important feature of orchid care. Orchids that have little or no fertiliser will not grow and will probably drop their old leaves as new ones develop. Ideally, you want a plant that grows bigger each year, putting on new leaves and one that is obviously looking healthy.

Generally speaking, fertiliser is fed to the plant by dissolving it into the water used for watering the plant. But one of the dangers of fertilising orchids can be that of fertiliser burn, through the use of too much fertiliser, which will cause the leaf tips to turn brown and can also cause root damage. So start by using half the recommended amount and see how your plant responds.

It is simple enough these days to purchase specialist orchid fertiliser. Alternatively, there are now fertilisers that come in spray bottles, which would be particular effective for feeding mounted orchids.

And more technical bits – fertilisers have three main components: nitrogen, phosphorus and potassium, and they are listed, as percentages by weight, in this order on the label. Nitrogen encourages the overall growth of plants; phosphorous is used to encourage flowering; and potassium is for root growth. Opinions vary, but look for a fertiliser than has approximately equal parts nitrogen and potassium with slightly less phosphorus, or equal amounts of all three.

Resting your plants

In its natural habitat, the orchid needs to have a rest period, which is provided by the change of seasons. In some instances, such as in an extremely hot, dry season, the plant becomes completely dormant, followed by a period of torrential rains, during which the plant appears to wake up and puts on new growth that culminates in flowering.

By watching your plants, you will learn to recognise their needs. When the plant feels the need of rest, and this usually occurs during the winter months, when light levels drop, active growth ceases, with no new roots or buds.

Most orchids cannot be persuaded to break this dormancy until they are ready, but others, if they are given conditions encouraging growth when they normally rest, will begin premature growth. If this happens, the flowers will not have a chance to mature and the plant will refuse to flower for a season. For a weak plant this may be a good idea, but of course, we usually want our orchids to flower every year.

When plants are resting and the roots are inactive, it is only natural that they should require little or no water. They usually need more air and less heat. In addition to these general rules, each of the genera, according to their native climate, has certain special needs.

For example, Cattleyas do not require complete rest: withholding water from the pot for a short time after re-potting or after flowering will be enough, but the bulbs should not be allowed to become dry to the point of shrivelling. The pot should be well watered and then allowed to dry out until the pot feels light in the hand.

Oncidium needs a long dry rest after a well-watered growing season. It lacks pseudobulbs, but the heavy, leathery leaves are capable of storing food and water for the dormant period. They enjoy a lack of water during the rest period, with only enough moisture to keep the bulbs from shrivelling.

Vanda is a pseudobulb-less genus. Growth is continuous. It appreciates warm, moist conditions, with slightly diminished water at the roots during winter. The genus Phalaenopsis is also pseudobulb-less, and, if properly nourished, will bloom constantly and never rest. But this tendency to too much activity must be limited or the plant will bloom itself to death. Buds can be pinched off, unless at least one pair of leaves have been formed since the last flowering. Old flower stems may break into bloom again, which weakens the plant and this should be discouraged by cutting stems close to the plant.

Odontoglossum, native to elevated parts of tropical Central America, requires no rest. The roots must be kept moist at all times, but care must be taken to prevent the compost from becoming stale.

Stanhopea, on the other hand, responds gratefully to a period of rest after growing. Rest can be encouraged by allowing the roots to dry out fairly well and by providing plenty of light and air. When new growth starts, you can start watering again generously. For most species blooming time comes in summer and should be immediately followed by a rest period.

These two chapters on the introduction to the growing conditions and the care of orchids may seem horribly complicated, but please don't be discouraged. Bear in mind, that if you buy one plant, then you will only have to consider the requirements of that one plant, whereas here I have covered the requirements of several different types of orchid.

But your orchid does need your attention, look at it carefully every day, notice any changes during its periods of both growth and rest, and you will soon begin to learn what it needs and when. In return, of course, you will be rewarded tenfold.

Figure 16 *Coelogyne cristata*

Moving on: Re-Potting Materials

Figure 17 *Dendrobium*

Having cared for your orchid successfully, there will come a time when you realise that the plant will now have to be re-potted, and this is a job that many new orchid growers are often reluctant to attempt. But there are certain signs that will be obvious when examining the plant that it is time to re-pot, such as when the bulbs look crowded together, hanging over the edge of the pots, or even pushing up into the air, and at this point, re-potting becomes crucial.

Another good reason for re-potting will be when the compost starts to decompose; the compost appears disintegrated and will feel soggy, it retains too much moisture and restricts air flow to the roots. To leave the plant in these conditions can result in the roots rotting and, ultimately, the demise of the plant.

It is important, therefore, to inspect the roots of your plant regularly to ensure that they are healthy, but if you find rather mushy, dead-looking roots , then it is time to re-pot.

Types of potting medium

The question of what is the most suitable material for potting orchids is a matter of considerable debate among orchid experts and there are probably as many orchid potting mixes as there are orchid growers.

The early English growers grew orchids successfully in sphagnum moss. Osmunda fibre was used extensively for a time, but because it became scarce, a number of other materials, including fir bark, gravel, and coconut husks were substituted, alone, or in combinations.

But to be quite honest, unless you want to take up orchid growing in a serious way, for example, for showing and competitions, then it is best for the beginner to purchase ready-made orchid compost from specialist suppliers, who can provide different combinations for the different species of orchid. But for interest's sake I will mention a few of the options available.

Orchid grade bark chippings: these come in different sizes, if the plant roots are thick choose a larger one, if they are small and thin then choose smaller chippings. They make a good general compost.

Lump peat and foam: this is a recent addition to the potting medium and is ideal for Phalaenopsis and those plants that need a little more moisture retention.

Sphagnum moss, bark and foam mix: a good starter for seedlings or very thinly rooted plants, but it will dry out very quickly, so be careful of under-watering.

Rock wool: usually rock wool is mixed with a little perlite. It is an inert medium, and certainly contains nothing to harm your plant roots, although always flush through very well when watering to avoid a build-up of salts. A disadvantage is that it can seem dry on the surface even when very wet underneath, and over time breaks down into a hard mass.

Equipment

Proper equipment is the next requirement for a successful re-potting operation. It is a good idea, when re-potting, to re-pot into a clear plastic plant pot. First, because you can see the roots growing and see any problems developing, and you can also see any pests that may have taken up residence in the pot. Second, Phalaenopsis orchids and others, which normally grow on things rather than in the ground, are used to having their roots exposed to light, so using clear pots will help them feel at home and encourage growth.

A disadvantage of using, for example, a clay pot, although this can be more stable than a plastic pot, is that the roots of the orchid do tend to stick to the clay. This makes re-potting a rather hazardous procedure, as the roots can easily become damaged as you try to prise them away from the pot.

However, you can also plant terrestrial orchids (that are used to having their roots in the dark) into a clear pot, which you can place inside a standard coloured pot, and you are then able to see at a glance if the roots need any attention.

Another option for some orchids, is to use baskets. These are especially suitable for orchids of the epiphytic type, such as Vanda, which if you consider their natural habitat, are perfectly happy, and indeed prefer, to have roots free to roam. And for Stanhopeas, whose flower spikes grow down through the potting medium, a basket is essential.

The downside of using a basket is that the roots can become entwined with the basket, but if re-potting is needed into a larger basket, then it is best to cut away as much of the old basket as possible before simply dropping it into the new, larger basket.

The type of container used, therefore, will depend on the need of the individual plant as well as, to a certain degree, your own taste. Pots are most suited to Cattleya and related types, as well as to Cymbidiums. Deeper containers are needed in hot and dry climates. Phalaenopsis can be grown in either pots or baskets. Oncidiums can thrive on rafts of bark or blocks of wood, in which case, the potting material can be tied firmly around the base of the plant and container with wire, allowing the air-loving roots to wander at will. Vanda, however, dislike the disturbance of being re-potted, and it may be best to simply remove the old compost carefully from between the roots with tweezers and gently replace with fresh.

Other equipment you will need is either a sharp knife or pair of cutters. Tweezers are also useful to remove any dead tissue from the bulbs and for taking out pieces of old compost from between the roots.

Before working with each plant, disinfect the tools, and use a fresh sheet of newspaper under each plant and pot. Being scrupulously clean will help protect the plants from contamination – cleanliness is important in re-potting. Old pots and crock (broken bits of pots used in the bottom of a pot for drainage) should be thoroughly scrubbed, and new pots should be soaked for a while before use.

How to re-pot an orchid

There are some general guidelines when it comes to re-potting orchids, and the first one to mention is, of course, not to re-pot the plant while it is in flower, as this will cause the plant too much stress. Wait until flowering has finished and ideally when the plant is starting to put on new growth. It is a good idea to soak the compost you are going to use overnight, so that it is thoroughly saturated before you start.

Another important consideration is to never over-pot, that is, don't automatically assume that you will need to use a larger pot. Orchids can manage in the same size pot for a considerable time and all that needs changing is the compost; in fact they prefer to be in slightly cramped conditions.

As a general guide to how often to re-pot:

- once a year: for Dendrobium, Miltonia, Paphiopedilum and Phalaenopsis;
- every second year: for Cattleya, Dendrobium, Oncidium, Odontoglossum;
- and every third year: for Vanda and Cymbidium.

Give yourself plenty of time, as re-potting your orchid is a procedure not to be hurried. First, take the plant gently out of the pot, and carefully clean away any old potting materials from around and between the roots. Also cut away any dead or shrivelled roots.

As mentioned above, it is a good idea to use a clear plastic pot. Put a few polystyrene chips or clean, broken pieces of clay at the bottom of the pot, which will create good air space and stop an accumulation of waterlogged compost at the base. Then add some of the potting medium you have chosen, set the plant in place, holding it steady while you pack the rest of the medium firmly, but gently, around the roots. Tap the pot on your work surface as you fill to help ensure that the medium drops down amongst the roots.

74

If the plant is not held firmly enough within the pot, it could move about and so damage its roots.

After re-potting, keep the plant in a warm place. Hold back on watering for a couple of weeks until the plant's roots have settled, but keep the humidity levels high.

Mounting orchids

There are some orchids, in particular epiphytes, that really do need air and room for their roots to roam, and mounting orchids on slabs of bark or twigs can be a natural way to grow them. Not only does this presentation look lovely, but many plants appreciate it and can flourish. They do require different treatment, however.

Because their roots are not held within a potting medium, mounted orchids need to be watered more frequently, although frequent misting may allow you to water a bit less often. A good way to water these plants is to submerge them into a bucket of water and leave them in there to soak for several minutes a couple times a week.

If you are growing mounted orchids, you need to make sure the humidity is high enough, so that the roots can also absorb moisture from the air. It can be helpful for sphagnum moss to be wrapped around the plant's roots to retain moisture for longer.

Re-potting mounted orchids can be a challenge, as you would probably have to destroy the roots to detach the plant from the old bark mount. However, what you can do is tie the old slab to a new one with fishing line or similar. If you're moving a plant from a pot to a slab, spread the roots out, add any moss you intend to use, then tie it all down with fishing line wrapped around the slab. You can remove the line once the plant has grown firmly in place.

Mounted plants are often grown with the slab of bark hung vertically, which can look particularly decorative if you have several hung together.

During re-potting is often a good time to start thinking about propagation – getting new, free plants – and I will look at that in the next chapter.

Want More Plants? Propagation

Figure 18 *Oncidium crispum*

Without a doubt, one of the most rewarding activities of any plant grower is that of propagation, getting new plants for free, and one that is especially applicable to orchids. However, a little care is needed to discover how best to propagate your particular orchid but some forms of orchid propagation are significantly easier than others.

Propagating orchids by division is straightforward, propagation from keikis is easy, but growing orchids from seed is quite tricky even for experienced orchid growers and, besides, can take a long time for the plant to reach flowering maturity (and for that reason, I am not going to cover growing from seed in this book).

Division

Plants of sympodial growth, that is with the new growth coming out of the base of, and alongside, the old bulbs, can easily be propagated by division. Cattleya and Cymbidium are typical of this type. Each year, the Cattleya adds a new growth at the front end of the plant, and certain species may occasionally grow in two and, occasionally, in three directions.

As the new bulbs form, the old ones often begin to lose their leaves and roots. They become what are known as 'poor relations', a burden on the living plant. Once separated from the living plant, the back-bulb, as these old dry bulbs are called, will, if placed in a warm, moist spot, start life over. After two, three, or perhaps four years, these will develop into new plants and will flower. The advantage of the back-bulb type of propagation over the growing from seed is that the flowers will exactly match those of the original plant.

If a monopodial orchid, such as a Vanda, has developed a branched stem, it can be carefully cut apart at the fork and both halves planted, though this is a more advanced orchid division technique, and some care will be required to make sure the half with few roots gets established successfully (extra humidity helps.) Though dividing monopodial orchids is a bit risky, it can be quite rewarding, since you now have two mature plants!

Keikis

Many orchids sometimes produce keikis, or small plantlets, either on their flower stems or along the canes of their pseudobulbs. Once they are mature enough, you can cut these off and pot them up to propagate your orchid. As with division, propagating orchids this way produces a clone of the parent plant; flowers will look identical.

Some types of orchids do this more readily than others. Phalaenopsis frequently propagate themselves by developing plantlets at the point where the flower falls off. Dendrobiums and other types develop them along their pseudobulbs, either at the tip of the pseudobulb or at the node above a leaf.

Dendrobium will grow little plantlets, complete with bulb and roots, quite readily, which develop from the cane-like flower stems. However, if you keep Dendrobiums too warm and moist during the dormant season, they will put their energy into plantlets and fail to bloom. (You can, if you are brave, do what many commercial growers do and pick the entire cane on flowering and, after cutting off the blooms, lay the canes on damp, warm sand or gravel to allow plantlets to develop from the dormant eyes.)

Once the new plant is sufficiently mature that the roots are a couple of inches long and it has at least a few leaves, you can carefully cut it off of the parent plant (use a sterile cutting tool such as a disposable razor blade, or a knife that you've soaked in bleach) Put the new plant into its own pot, basket, or on its own slab, following the instructions given in the previous chapter on re-potting orchids. It may well be a couple of years before it starts to flower, although keeping the new plant attached to its parent for longer may help it develop to flowering size more quickly.

Pruning

I just quickly want to cover the subject of pruning orchids because, in fact, unlike other plants or shrubs that can be cut back to encourage bushy growth, orchids don't like being cut back.

However, trimming orchids to remove old leaves and flower stems is a good idea and if done properly, can remove the old plant tissue that would decay and potentially spread rot to the rest of the plant. Sometimes old dead tissue can also harbour insect pests, as well as it being just plain unsightly.

Trim off any dead tissue you find on a plant: old flower stems (but not those that are still green as these may re-flower, particularly in the case of Phalaenopsis), old leaves, any old rotting pseudobulbs, or dead roots found when re-potting. If just a leaf's tip has died back, cut off just the dead part, or perhaps a few millimetres into the green part if the dieback seems to be progressing.

Remember that if there is still some green in the stem, then it is not dead!

In many cases of orchid disease, particularly bacterial and fungal infections, it's a good idea to trim off the affected tissue, and slightly past it into healthy tissue. This can stop the progression of the disease.

Only use sterile cutting tools when trimming orchids. Otherwise, you can spread disease, possibly including incurable viruses, from one plant to another. So either use disposable razors, or soak your tools in disinfectant.

And talking of diseases, that is what I am going to be looking at in the next chapter.

What Can Go Wrong?

Figure 19 *Vanda insignis*

There are several types of orchid disease: pests are fairly common, as well as fungi, moulds and viruses that can attack orchids. Orchids can also be affected by various types of environmental damage such as that caused by inappropriate temperatures and watering, much of which can be prevented by better orchid care and attention.

But let's look at some of the problems that an orchid grower can face and how best to deal with them.

Viruses

Viruses are the most widespread disease problems affecting orchids but fortunately most of them are rare, and in many cases hardly cause symptoms. There are several kinds of viruses, and different viruses affect different types of orchids.

However, identifying the specific type of virus is not particularly helpful as they are all incurable. The viruses can appear as discolouration, irregular markings on the leaves or uneven patches on the flowers, usually of dead, brown tissue. Sadly, all you can do once a virus has infected your plant is to either discard the plant or isolate it from the rest of your collection.

To avoid spreading orchid viruses – and I can't emphasis this enough – it is vital that you sterilise any cutting tools you use on your orchids. You can do this with disinfectant, or in a flame. You can also use disposable razor blades that you throw away after tending each plant. Sterilising tools should be done any time you trim orchids, such as when removing old roots in re-potting, or when dividing orchids.

Pests

It's always a good idea to carefully check any new plants you have bought for pests before adding them to your collection. Some growers provide a separate quarantine area for new plants, keeping them there for a month or two so they can monitor the plant for pests, diseases, and weeds. A few of these beasties are:

Scale insects: These bugs have tiny larvae that crawl around your plant and then as adults, hiding under a scaly covering, they latch onto the plant and start sucking its juices. Although pesticides will work against them, most don't work that well because of the protection that the scales give the insects. You could use an insecticidal soap that will stick to them and which can be effective. The best approach, though, is to rub them off with a cotton swab dipped in alcohol or methylated spirits, then spray a conventional insecticide on the plant.

Mealy bugs: Another sap-sucking insect that likes to hide in hard-to-reach places on the plant. Treat them much like scale insects.

Aphids: These insects crawl around a plant, sucking its sap, often exuding a sticky secretion. They are particularly fond of flower stems. They're pretty easy to defeat. If there are just a few, the most effective way is to simply remove them by hand, squishing them between your fingers. Most pesticides will work, and I've had good luck with a spray bottle containing diluted detergent.

Spider-mites: These are tiny insects and not spiders at all, but get their name from the 'web' they spin to protect the eggs, which are usually hidden on the underside of the leaves. Use a cotton bud soaked in methylated spirits to wipe the leaves, and repeat every couple of days until the plant is clear.

Slugs and Snails: Even if your plants are inside your home, there is a good chance that these enterprising creatures will find a way in. They are easily recognised by their slime trails and you will see holes appearing in the leaves of your plants. As they appear mostly at night, you could organise a midnight raid and simply pick them off and squish them! Alternatively, you could scatter a couple of slug pellets in the pots and this will kill them.

Bacterial and fungal infections

There are many possible bacterial and fungal infections of orchids and are most common in plants that are being over-watered (for example, root rot) or whose foliage is often wet. Repeated misting of the plants can cause the latter problem, as can letting water settle into the crown of a plant (to which Phalaenopsis are especially vulnerable, since the configuration of the leaves prevents the water from draining away).

To help prevent rot, it is best to avoid over-watering; aim to water plants early in the day as they will tend to dry more quickly when there is still plenty of light and temperatures are warmer. Also make sure there is plenty of air circulation.

If the plant has leaf rot, cut off the infected part of the leaf. Crown rot also requires cutting off the infected tissue, though this is hard, since that is the plant's growth tip and it may take a long time to recover. For root rot, re-pot the plant, taking care to trim off all dead and dying roots. Though orchids don't like being cut back, pruning to remove diseased tissue may save the plant's life.

Sometimes fungal diseases can affect orchid flowers, resulting in types of brown spotting. Remove affected flowers and, if you have caught it in time, it won't spread to the rest. Also be sure to discard the flower stem promptly when the plant finishes flowering.

Over-watering and under-watering

Under-watering tends to result in orchid plants losing leaves, as most orchids don't wilt when they are dry: however, the pseudobulbs will shrivel. The new growth may fail to expand properly and have a pleated appearance, either lengthways or vertical to the leaf's central crease.

Or the plant may simply be too weak and fail to bloom.

Over-watering can produce similar symptoms to under-watering: it can cause the roots to rot, or the potting mix breaks down. But in either case, the plant is unable to get enough water.

The best way to determine whether under-watering or over-watering is the culprit, inspect the root system to find out if it's rotten; try to lift the plant out of the pot with its potting mix to look at the roots. Clear plastic pots make monitoring root health easier, and I would recommend using them.

If the root system is in bad shape, re-pot the orchid, removing all the old, dead roots. If it has few roots left, you may want to raise the humidity to help it recover.

Sunburn and fertiliser burn

If the leaves of your orchid are exposed to too much sunlight, they can overheat, and those parts of the leaf will die, leaving brown or black marks. This damage is generally irreversible and the best thing to do is reduce the amount of light the plant receives. For example, move the plant further away from a sunny window, or ensure the light is filtered through a blind or curtain.

However, sunburn happens most frequently when the plant is taken outside for the summer and gets too much direct sunlight. Ensure that it is situated where it can be shaded from midday sun.

If the tips of the leaves turn brown, this can sometimes be due to too much fertiliser, or to fertiliser salts having built up in the orchid's potting mix. In the latter case, simply re-pot and make sure to flush the plant with water regularly to prevent salt build-up in the future. Of course, if you're over-fertilising, use less. The general rule for orchids is to fertilise 'weakly, weekly'.

I know this chapter will give the impression that there are a whole host of problems awaiting your orchid. But if you give your plants a quick check over regularly, you will help prevent any of the above taking serious hold.

Conclusion: Now It's Up to You!

My intention with this book has been to give you the essential information you need to start growing and caring for your first orchids. You will appreciate that there are, of course, many aspects of orchid growing that I have not covered, such as growing under greenhouse conditions.

But the reason for that is I wanted to keep it simple. I wanted to provide straightforward information that would enable anyone who is interested in orchids to grow and care for one or more of these amazing plants. And I wanted to look specifically at those orchids that are suitable to be grown as house plants, so that you could really enjoy your orchids at close quarters.

My aim has been to motivate, inspire and encourage you to take the first steps in growing orchids – I do hope that I have done just that.

Enjoy!

Figure 20 *Cymbidium insigne*

A Quick Reference Guide

What follows is a summary of the main points of the book, a sort of quick reference or 'cheat sheet', covering the most suitable first orchids for anyone to look after, with their primary requirements.

Phalaenopsis, or more commonly known as the moth orchid, is readily available and is absolutely the number-one best orchid houseplant.

- Light: no direct sunlight, either an east or west facing or shaded window.
- Heat: requires temperatures in the day around 70°–85°F (20°–30°C), and a fall in temperature of around 10°–15° at night. Provide good air circulation but no direct draughts.
- Water: take care not to let water sit in the crown of the plant, and do not allow the plant to dry out.

- Rest: could bloom constantly, but this will weaken the plant, so cut flower stems close to the base after flowering.

Cattleya is one of the easiest orchids to care for and is extremely popular because of its beautiful large blooms.

- Light: quite high; a south facing window in the northern hemisphere, but avoid midday sun.
- Heat: requires temperatures in the day around 70°–85°F (20°–30°C), and a fall in temperature of around 10°–15° at night. Provide good air circulation but no direct draughts.
- Water: must be allowed to dry out between waterings. Soak the pot thoroughly and allow to drain.
- Rest: reduce watering slightly after flowering for a short period, but do not allow the pseudobulbs to dry out.

Dendrobium, with so many different species, care requirements can differ, although the most common plants available are usually hybrids of Den. *phalaenopsis*.

- Light: they like bright light, either an east, west or lightly shaded south facing window.

- Heat: requires temperatures in the day around 70°–85°F (20°–30°C), and a fall in temperature of around 10°–15° at night. Provide good air circulation but no direct draughts.

- Water: keep this plant evenly moist during growth, but allow to dry between waterings after growth is mature.

- Rest: A short, three to four week rest with a lower temperature, then grown warmer again, will encourage new growth.

Paphiopedilum, often called the slipper orchid, or lady's slipper orchid, are quite easy to grow indoors.

- Light: they enjoy bright light, but will not tolerate direct sun, so an east facing window is ideal.

- Heat: these plants require temperatures that we would be comfortable with, between 60° and 75°F (15°–25°C) during the day and a night-time drop of around 10°F. Provide good air circulation but no direct draughts.

- Water: keep evenly moist but not wet, and water before the plant dries out.

- Rest: a cool winter rest is recommended for this plant, reducing watering and lowering night-time temperatures by a few degrees.

Oncidium, sometimes referred to as the dancing lady orchid, are not quite so easy to please for new growers, but are well worth any extra care.

- Light: will grow in bright light, but require some shading from direct sun, especially in the summer months.

- Heat: these plants require temperatures that we would be comfortable with, between 60° and 75°F (15°–25°C) during the day and a night-time drop of around 10°F.

Provide good air circulation but no direct draughts.

- Water: keep evenly moist but not wet, and water before the plant dries out.
- Rest: they need less water during their rest period, but not so little that the bulbs start to shrivel.

Cymbidium is one of the best known orchids and is much more cold tolerant than many of the more common species. It is frequently grown outside in the summer months in temperate climates.

- Light: they enjoy morning and evening sun, but will need to be placed in the shade to protect from the midday sun.
- Heat: they prefer day-time temperatures of around 50°–70°F (10°–20°C), with a drop at night of about 15°F. Some can even tolerate a temperature as low as 40°F.
- Air: good air movement is essential for Cymbidiums, and they appreciate being outside in the summer months.

- Water: keep the compost moist and never allow the plants to dry out.

- Rest: they need cooler temperatures during late autumn to initiate new flower growths, so reduce watering during this time.

General advice

There is some general advice that can be applied to all types of orchids, and in particular:

Humidity: orchids prefer high humidity, so place the plant pot on a tray of pebbles half filled with water, ensuring the roots do not sit in the water. Be careful in winter, as humidity levels can drop dramatically as the central heating is used far more. Grouping plants together can increase the humidity. You can also mist spray the plant frequently, and aerial roots will appreciate this particularly, but make sure you do this in the morning to allow the plant leaves to dry.

Watering: generally it is best to take the plant to the sink and run the water through it to thoroughly soak the potting medium, but be sure to allow the excess water to drain away.

Temperature: Most of the commonly available orchids are chosen to make growing orchids for beginners easy, which means that if your plant came from a supermarket or orchid mass-market place, it will probably do well in temperatures that are comfortable for humans.

Glossary

Deciduous: sheds leaves at the end of the growing season.

Distichous: leaves arranged in two vertical rows on opposite sides of a stem.

Epiphytic: a plant growing on another plant for support, but not taking its nutrients from that plant.

Genus (pl. genera): a group of **species** exhibiting similar characteristics.

Hybrid: the offspring of breeding plants that are of different **species.**

Monopodial: growing continuously from a central crown.

Node: the point on a plant stem where the leaf or flower is produced.

Panicles: a branched cluster of flowers.

Pseudobulb: a bulb-like fleshy stem and used for storage.

Racemes: flowers are borne along a main stem, the oldest flowers at the base

Rhizome: a creeping horizontal stem used for reproduction and storage

Sepal: a modified leaf that, in orchids, closely resembles the petals

Species: a plant that is a natural member of a **genus** rather than a **hybrid**

Sympodial: new growth appears from the **rhizome** alongside the previous year's growth

Terrestrial: a plant that grows on land rather than in water or on trees or rocks.

Picture Credits

Plates:

Figure: 1: Laelia jongheana, a botanical illustration from the *Dictionnaire Iconographique des Orchidees*, 1896.

Figure 4: Cymbidium grandiflorum, a botanical illustration from the *Dictionnaire Iconographique des Orchidees*, 1896. Also available at http://orchid.unibas.ch.

Figure 5: *Orchids and Hummingbirds*, painting by Martin Johnson Heade (1819–1904), showing an epiphyte orchid growing on a tree.

Figure 6: Laelia superbiens, this plate shows part of the hand-retouched chromolithograph after a drawing by Miss S. A. Drake (fl. 1820–40s), from James Bateman (1811–97) *The Orchidaceae of Mexico and Guatemala*.

Figure 18: Oncidium crispum, this illustration is from *The Botanist*, founded in 1837, a sister periodical to the successful *Botanic Garden*.

Figures: Frontispiece, 2, 8, 10, 12, 13, 14, 16, 19 and 20: These beautiful botanical drawings have come from *Curtis's Botanical Magazine.* This magazine was begun in 1787 by William Curtis and is the longest running botanical magazine, continuing to be published today by the Royal Botanic Gardens, Kew. In many cases, the detail of the plants can be seen more clearly than in some modern photographs, as well as showing just how varied orchid flowers can be, even within the same species.

Photographs:

Figure 11: Vanda in hanging basket, courtesy of blumenbiene from Flickr.

Figure 15: Miltonia, courtesy of Sheetha from Flickr.

Figure 17: White Dendrobium, courtesy of blumenbiene from Flickr.

Figures 3, 7, 9: many thanks to those photographers who made their work available under the Creative Commons, Universal Public Domain Dedication.

About the Author

Fran Barnwell (the pen name of author Linda McGrory) has been providing gardening advice for beginners for many years through her website http://www.newtogardening.co.uk.

Fran's philosophy is to provide simple and straightforward advice for anyone starting out with gardening, whether that is indoors or outdoors, with a good-sized garden or just a window ledge. *How to Grow Orchids* is the second book in The New to Gardening Series. The second edition of *How to Start Gardening: A Step by Step Guide for Beginners* is to be published in September 2012.

Made in United States
North Haven, CT
23 May 2024

52861849R00059